Business & The Bible
Matthew 25

Tamara Diahann

Copyright © 2015 Tamara Diahann

All rights reserved.

ISBN: 1511636904
ISBN-13:978-1511636902

Contents

Welcome — **Page 3**

Day 1: Matthew 25:1-13 — **Page 5**
Prepare for the Future of Your Business NOW

Day 2: Matthew 25:14-15 — **Page 9**
According To Your Ability

Day 3: Matthew 25:16-18 — **Page 13**
Use What You Have To Get What You Want

Key Verse & Prayer Cards — **Page 16**

Day 4: Matthew 25:19-30 — **Page 24**
Don't Be Surprised If You Lose Your Market Share

Day 5: Matthew 25:31-46 — **Page 28**
A Call to Give

Personal Inventory — **Page 33**

Hello there fellow Christian Over-Achiever,

Your BOSS Exec Tamara Diahann here.... Thank you so much for joining me on this journey through Matthew 25.

To be honest, I'm tired of nonbelievers having more faith, doing more, making more money, and making more notable change in this world than I am. As believers we are suppose to be heirs and joint heirs with Jesus Christ. We have the purest most majestic power living inside of us and yet we often live mediocre pitiful lives. All because we fail to activate and be dedicated to the power that is the Holy Spirit.

As business owners we often look to the world for advice on how to make more money, how to build our brands, and how to reach our fullest potential. And although these resources are helpful, they should only be supplements (not main sources) to that which we learn from the Word of God.

Such is the purpose of the Business & the Bible Devotional series. If you are reading this you obviously realize the need for daily quiet time with God. So why not turn it into a time to learn not only what God's words says but how to effectively apply it to your daily life.

There are no secrets to success within these pages. Just simple practical suggestions on how to live out God's word. And I pray it blesses you immensely.

Sending you positive vibes and the Love of Christ,
-Tamara Diahann

Connect With Me

IG @BOSS_Exec
www.Facebook.com/TamaraisBOSS
TamaraisBOSS@gmail.com
#BOSS4Christ

Prepare for the Future of Your Business NOW

Matthew 25:1-13

"Then the Kingdom of Heaven will be like ten bridesmaids who took their lamps and went to meet the bridegroom. **2** Five of them were foolish, and five were wise. **3** The five who were foolish didn't take enough olive oil for their lamps, **4** but the other five were wise enough to take along extra oil. **5** When the bridegroom was delayed, they all became drowsy and fell asleep. **6** "At midnight they were roused by the shout, 'Look, the bridegroom is coming! Come out and meet him!' **7** "All the bridesmaids got up and prepared their lamps. **8** Then the five foolish ones asked the others, 'Please give us some of your oil because our lamps are going out.' **9** "But the others replied, 'We don't have enough for all of us. Go to a shop and buy some for yourselves.' **10** "But while they were gone to buy oil, the bridegroom came. Then those who were ready went in with him to the marriage feast, and the door was locked. **11** Later, when the other five bridesmaids returned, they stood outside, calling, 'Lord! Lord! Open the door for us!' **12** "But he called back, 'Believe me, I don't know you!' **13** "So you, too, must keep watch! For you do not know the day or hour of my return.

Points to Ponder

Many of us have started a business with a clear objective in mind; we gather all that we think we need for the moment; and start on our merry way meticulously waiting for the perfect opportunity. But sometimes that opportunity's arrival may take a bit longer than planned. And like the foolish virgins in this passage, when it finally presents itself, we have run through all our allotted resources and cannot seize it. So we scrambled to pull things together and in the process it literally passes us by and the door is shut. If this sounds like you, you are not alone. The good news is, no matter how long you have been in business or how many opportunities you have missed due to being ill prepared, because you have breath in your body there is still time to become like the wise virgins. It's going to take changing of some habits which may be difficult at times. But it will be worth it.

Application

1. Think about the current status of your business. What is one goal you would like to accomplish over the next 2 weeks? *Note make sure that is is SMART (**S**pecific, **M**easurable, **A**ctionable, **R**ealistic, and **T**ime-sensitive)*

2. Identify what resources you currently have that can help you achieve this goal.

3. What resources do you need in order to achieve it?

4. Identify what you need to have in place in the event your goal takes longer than 2 weeks to achieve.

5. How does this goal help advance the Kingdom of God?

6. Create your 2 week action plan.

7. Execute your plan

Prayer

Awesome and amazing God, you know what we need before we ask it. Thank you for your wisdom and love. Please forgive us for starting businesses, projects, initiatives, ministries and everything else without first counting up the cost. For so long we have been like the foolish virgins running out of resources before you choose to show up. Forgive us for this oh Lord. And help us to lean and depend on the wisdom and understanding that your Holy Spirit gives. So that we will be able to accomplish those things you have willed for us to do for your glory and honor. In Jesus name we pray. AMEN

Write Your Personal Prayer

_____
_____
_____
_____

Key Verse
But while they were gone to buy oil, the groom came. Those who were ready went with him into the wedding. Then the door was shut. *Matthew 25:10*

Affirmation
I am well equipped to achieve my goals no matter how long they may take..

According To Your Ability

Matthew 25:14-15
14 "Again, the Kingdom of Heaven can be illustrated by the story of a man going on a long trip. He called together his servants and entrusted his money to them while he was gone. **15** He gave five bags of silver to one, two bags of silver to another, and one bag of silver to the last—dividing it in proportion to their abilities. He then left on his trip.

Point To Ponder
Have you ever wondered why you had this vision of a grand profitable business, but (as my mother would say), "didn't have two nickels to rub together", let alone finance the start of a company? Has this ever made you question why God gave you the vision in the first place? Or made you wonder if it really was from God? Were you just fooling yourself into thinking you were made to do something great? I ask myself these questions often. Because I too wonder why such a desire to be great was put in me with no signs of how I'd get the necessary resources to get there. In one of these seasons of questioning I came upon Matthew 25:14-15. And the latter part of verse 15 really hit home. "He gave according to that servant's ability." What a punch in the gut. I was like "Wait a minute Lord… So you mean to tell me, that I have so little because of my inability to handle much?!?" Geezzz, that sucks, I thought. But then the more I considered this verse the more it forced me to examine myself. And here is what I found:

1. My spending habits were less than desirable. So even if He (God) gave me every monetary resource I needed to build my enterprise. Him and I both knew I wouldn't spend it currently.

2. I was walking into a new industry, a new business model, one I had to learn the ends and outs myself before I could properly train and solicit help. I mean I really learned a lot doing the things I needed in order to run my business that I didn't have the money to pay someone to do. Like, designing my magazine; creating

engaging event pages/events; using online meeting and booking tools; creating a membership site; the list goes on.

3. My market is Christians, who love God, have started a business through faith, and needed encouragement that they have made the right choice. As well as the resources, guidance, and support to grow into something greater. Therefore, I too had to live out such a faith walk in order to effectively bring about change in the lives of those I serve.

So after further consideration, I reluctantly (because who actually wants to admit they have room to grow) agree with God. He truly gave according to my ability and as much as I hate to say it, I have learned so much as I use what He has given me for the progress, growth, and advancement of my company.

What about you?

Application

1. Do you believe God has accurately given to you according to your ability? Why or Why not?

2. Identify 2-3 things that you have learned about yourself and/or your business as you utilize the resources you were given.
3. How would you and/or your business be different had you not learned these lessons and skills?

4. Are there any additional opportunities for growth both in Christ and as a business owner that your current revenue or lack thereof is allotting you? If so, what are they?

5. How will you use your situation to grow in these areas?

Prayer

Dear Lord, you are all knowing. Your ways are not our ways and your thoughts as not our thoughts. You knew the ending even before the beginning. And your wisdom exceeds us all. You are the creator of all and you promised you would never put more on us than we can bear. Now Lord forgive us for we often only consider this promise when it comes to bad things. But you know our current abilities, and you know how much of your possessions (for all is yours to give) we can handle at this point in time. Forgive us of our ignorance and if there has been anytime when we've doubted your wisdom. But Lord, help us to positively pursue opportunities for growth and to welcome them with open arms knowing that we are going to be better, wiser, and able to handle more once we learn what it is we are to learn. In the mighty name of Jesus I pray and thank you. Amen.

Write Your Personal Prayer

_____
_____
_____
_____

Key Verse

He gave to each servant according to that servant's ability. Then he left on his journey. *Matthew 25:15b*

Affirmation

What I have now is preparing me for what I'm going to have in the future. I welcome the opportunity for spiritual and professional growth as I apply what I do have to my business for the progress, growth, and advancement of the Kingdom of God.

Personal Inventory… Have you been applying what you've learned so far into your daily life? If so how? If not what can you do to start today?

_____
_____
_____
_____
_____
_____
_____
_____
_____
_____
_____
_____
_____
_____
_____
_____

Use What You Have To Get What You Want

Matthew 25:16-18

16 The servant who had the five pieces of money went out to the stores and traded until he made five more pieces. **17** The servant who had two pieces of money did the same thing. He made two more pieces. **18** The servant who had received the one piece of money went and hid the money in a hole in the ground. He hid his owner's money.

Point To Ponder

How many times have you said something like this...

"Lord, if you just give me a little more money I would...?" I too am guilty so trust me as I write today's devotion I too am convicted. I often pity myself for the lack of resources I have to run my business, and often waste my time dreaming about when I will have more than enough to do and buy whatever I want and need. But you and I both know nothing gets done simply by dreaming. So instead, I have committed to be like the servant with the five pieces of money or the one with two pieces even and use what I currently have to make more.

What about you?

Application

1. Are you willing to trust God to add increase to what you do have when you diligently work on your business? Why? or Why not?

2. If so, complete the chart to help you map out how this commitment translates into your daily activity?

I currently have...	I will use it to...	My goal is to...	I believe God will...

3. Choose at least one resource from the list you made above to focus on this week to express your new found confidence in God.

Prayer

Dear all knowing and loving God. You know just what we need to accomplish the tasks you have set before us. You know that when you give us too much we misplace our faith in those things instead of in you. Please help us to activate faith by diligently working on our businesses with the certainty that like the servant with five pieces of money and the one with two that you will bring the increase. Please help us to avoid fear, laziness, and self pity all of which will cause us not to use what we have to bring you glory. Father, let our businesses growth be a living testimony of how you are the Holy Provider able to do exceedingly, abundantly, above all we can ask or think. In Jesus name I pray, AMEN.

Write Your Personal Prayer

_____
_____
_____
_____
_____
_____
_____
_____

Key Verse

16 The servant who had the five pieces of money went out to the stores and traded until he made five more pieces. *Matthew 25:16*

Affirmation

I trust God to add increase to what I do have when I diligently work on my business?

"But while they were gone to buy oil, the bridegroom came. Then those who were ready went in with him to the marriage feast, and the door was locked.
Matthew 25:10

He gave five bags of silver to one, two bags of silver to another, and one bag of silver to the last—dividing it in proportion to their abilities. He then left on his trip.
Matthew 25:15

"The servant who received the five bags of silver began to invest the money and earned five more.
Matthew 25:16

To those who use well what they are given, even more will be given, and they will have an abundance. But from those who do nothing, even what little they have will be taken away.
Matthew 25:29

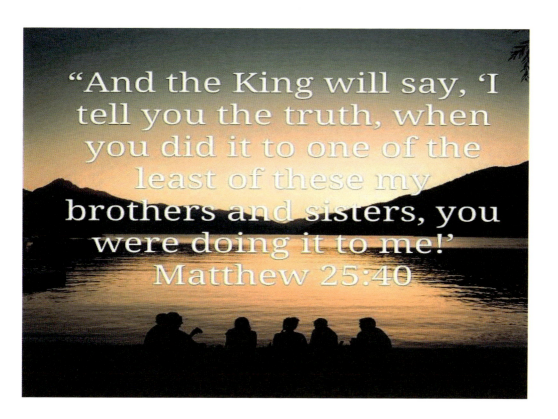

"And the King will say, 'I tell you the truth, when you did it to one of the least of these my brothers and sisters, you were doing it to me!' Matthew 25:40

Prayer Request:

Date Requested:

Answer:

Date Answered:

Prayer Request:

Date Requested:

Answer:

Date Answered:

Prayer Request:

Date Requested:

Answer:

Date Answered:

Don't Be Surprised If You Lose Your Market Share

Matthew 25:19-30

19 "After a long time their master returned from his trip and called them to give an account of how they had used his money. **20** The servant to whom he had entrusted the five bags of silver came forward with five more and said, 'Master, you gave me five bags of silver to invest, and I have earned five more.' **21** "The master was full of praise. 'Well done, my good and faithful servant. You have been faithful in handling this small amount, so now I will give you many more responsibilities. Let's celebrate together! **22** "The servant who had received the two bags of silver came forward and said, 'Master, you gave me two bags of silver to invest, and I have earned two more.' **23** "The master said, 'Well done, my good and faithful servant. You have been faithful in handling this small amount, so now I will give you many more responsibilities. Let's celebrate together!' **24** "Then the servant with the one bag of silver came and said, 'Master, I knew you were a harsh man, harvesting crops you didn't plant and gathering crops you didn't cultivate. **25** I was afraid I would lose your money, so I hid it in the earth. Look, here is your money back.' **26** "But the master replied, 'You wicked and lazy servant! If you knew I harvested crops I didn't plant and gathered crops I didn't cultivate, **27** why didn't you deposit my money in the bank? At least I could have gotten some interest on it.' **28** "Then he ordered, 'Take the money from this servant, and give it to the one with the ten bags of silver. **29** To those who use well what they are given, even more will be given, and they will have an abundance. But from those who do nothing, even what little they have will be taken away. **30** Now throw this useless servant into outer darkness, where there will be weeping and gnashing of teeth.'

Points To Ponder

It's a simple concept really. But a difficult one to put into practice. Even if you have what you would consider a little, you must still put it to work. Otherwise, God will take what you do have from you and give it to someone else.

The same goes for growing your business. If you do not diligently work on and in it sooner or later some similar business will come and take your market share meaning your customers (both current and potential); your social media following; etc. So be mindful to work on marketing your business and offering high quality products and services daily.

Application

1. Think about the one resource from your list that you committed to focus on to express your confidence in God's ability to bring increase.

2. Rewrite it in the space below:

I currently have...	I will use it to...	My goal is to...	I believe God will...

3. Now create a monthly, weekly, and daily checklist of action items utilizing that resources for the purpose of achieving your set goal.

4. Write your commit to executing this plan for the next 40 days.

Prayer

Lord, mighty and all knowing Father in heaven. Please help me to diligently work towards growing my business. Let my daily put to work the resources you have so graciously given that I may bring you glory and honor. And also so I can experience the manifestation of the promises laid out in your word; that I will in fact be given more to the point of abundance if I use well what I currently have. And Lord, forgive me for not doing so before and blaming you for the digression of my projects, business, and quality of life. In Jesus name I pray AMEN.

Write Your Personal Prayer

_____
_____
_____
_____
_____

Key Verse

Those who use well what they are given more will be given, and they will have an abundance. But for those who do nothing even what little they have will be taken away. Matthew 25:29 NLT

Affirmation

I will continue to bring God glory by working on and in my business daily and increasing my market share.

Additional Action Checklist Planning Space

A Call To Give

Matthew 25:31-46
31 "But when the Son of Man comes in his glory, and all the angels with him, then he will sit upon his glorious throne. 32 All the nations will be gathered in his presence, and he will separate the people as a shepherd separates the sheep from the goats. 33 He will place the sheep at his right hand and the goats at his left. 34 "Then the King will say to those on his right, 'Come, you who are blessed by my Father, inherit the Kingdom prepared for you from the creation of the world. 35 For I was hungry, and you fed me. I was thirsty, and you gave me a drink. I was a stranger, and you invited me into your home. 36 I was naked, and you gave me clothing. I was sick, and you cared for me. I was in prison, and you visited me.' 37 "Then these righteous ones will reply, 'Lord, when did we ever see you hungry and feed you? Or thirsty and give you something to drink? 38 Or a stranger and show you hospitality? Or naked and give you clothing? 39 When did we ever see you sick or in prison and visit you?' 40 "And the King will say, 'I tell you the truth, when you did it to one of the least of these my brothers and sisters,you were doing it to me!' 41 "Then the King will turn to those on the left and say, 'Away with you, you cursed ones, into the eternal fire prepared for the devil and his demons. 42 For I was hungry, and you didn't feed me. I was thirsty, and you didn't give me a drink. 43 I was a stranger, and you didn't invite me into your home. I was naked, and you didn't give me clothing. I was sick and in prison, and you didn't visit me.' 44 "Then they will reply, 'Lord, when did we ever see you hungry or thirsty or a stranger or naked or sick or in prison, and not help you?' 45 "And he will answer, 'I tell you the truth, when you refused to help the least of these my brothers and sisters, you were refusing to help me.' 46 "And they will go away into eternal punishment, but the righteous will go into eternal life."

Point to Ponder
Running a business is not for the faint of heart... we all know this. But sometimes we can get so consumed with trying to grow our business that we forget that our ultimate purpose and quite frankly only purpose in life is

to bring God glory. And we do so BECAUSE we love Him and BY loving others as ourselves. But we must not just say we love, we must show it. And believe it or not, because we are business owners, we have a lot more freedom to do so than we realize. Our businesses are literally our ministries.

Use Matthew 25:34-36 to help you determine just how you can use your products and/or services to help those in need. Can they be used to help the hungry? Clothed the naked? Serve the underprivileged or members of your church? You don't have to go out and start your own non-profit or run a large campaign in order to do so either. The scripture shows that God honors those who simply recognizes a need and meets it.

Application

1. Identify at least 1-3 community based organization in your area that you can partner with. Ideally, these organizations should have goals and missions cohesive with your business and market.

    Name of organization:

    Who do they serve:

    Website:

    Point of Contact:

    Email:

    Phone:

    Name of organization:

    Who do they serve:

    Website:

Point of Contact:

Email:

Phone:

Name of organization:

Who do they serve:

Website:

Point of Contact:

Email:

Phone:

2. Make a list of your services, skills, and/or products that you can offer them on at least a monthly bases to meet a need those they serve or the organization as a whole might have.

3. Contact each group and commit yourself to service. Write your commitment in the space provided.

Prayer

Lord, please forgive us for being so selfish. We often times think we don't have enough for ourselves so we fail to give. But Lord you have given us time, talent, and treasure through our businesses that we can use to meet a specific need in our communities. Help us to step out on faith and just do without reservation. And Lord please also help us to stay committed to it and grow in faith and dedication to serve you as we serve others. In Jesus name I pray AMEN!

Write Your Personal Prayer

_____

_____

_____

_____

_____

Key Verse

Then the King will reply to them, I assure you that when you have done it for one of the least of these brothers and sisters of mine, you have done it for me. Matthew 25:40

Affirmation

I have more than enough. Therefore, I will give and meet the needs of my community.

Congratulations you have completed your first Business & The Bible Devotional

Personal Inventory

Devotion Topics:
1.
2.
3.
4.
5.

Devotion Affirmations:
1.

2.

3.

4.

5.

Which topics have I made a genuine effort to apply to my life? Why do I think this is so?

Which topics are still opportunities for Spiritual Growth? Why do I think this is so?

What have I learned about God and/or myself by completing this devotional?

How have I experienced God move in my life while completing this devotional?

How did I work towards the achievement of the goals I was prompted to set?

I'm I working diligently to achieve them? Why or why not?

Write a personal prayer.

Closing Thoughts

Made in the USA
Lexington, KY
28 May 2016